AF521774

That Other Beauty

That Other Beauty

Karen Enns

Brick Books

Library and Archives Canada Cataloguing in Publication

Enns, Karen, 1960-
That Other Beauty / Karen Enns.

Poems.
ISBN 978-1-894078-80-1

I. Title.

PS8609.N57T53 2010 C811'.6 C2010-903704-9

We acknowledge the Canada Council for the Arts, the Government of Canada through the Book Publishing Industry Development Program (BPIDP), and the Ontario Arts Council for their support of our publishing program.

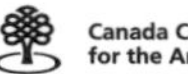

Canadä
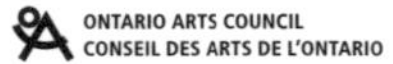

Cover art: Lorraine Thorarinson Betts, *Beyond Us All*, 2008, mixed media oil on paper.

The author photograph was taken by Arthur Rowe.

The book is set in AG Buch and Sabon.

Design and layout by Alan Siu.

Printed and bound by Sunville Printco Inc.

Brick Books
431 Boler Road, Box 20081
London, Ontario N6K 4G6

www.brickbooks.ca

In memory of

Franz Janzen (1911 - 1998)

Eleonore Janzen (1918 - 2008)

Contents

I

II

III

Give us astonishment
and a flame, high, bright.

– Adam Zagajewski

I

Crossing the Border

A moment's hesitation
and you're standing on the dirt road with the pear trees
breaking at the side and berries you don't know the name of
in your hand. You've heard the wells are dry
and now you see the ditches too.
And there are low stone walls around the orchards,
the dwindling art of squatters
in the field: empty baskets, jugs,
old boards and rope.
There are birds.
But you've been here before. In the grass,
your shoes, your notebook, pen.
Under the leaves, the wooden seat,
the path that takes you there
still narrow, bright.

The Hand Is a Field of Grasses

> The heart is three bowls
> always full and one empty.
> The heart is a four-winged
> bird as it lifts and unfolds.
> – from *Sutra of the Heart*,
> Robert Bringhurst

The hand is a field of grasses
in the laid-down light of day.
The hand is the bark of willow and pear, white poplar
and birch. The hand is water, rain-barrelled luck
or the flame of thirst.

The hand is fire, licked clean, snapped
and given off as warmth.
The hand is wood, stone, cloth,
the lamplight, needle, thread.

The hand is the land, the black dirt
turned up soft in spring and loam and clay
and the deep, dark thigh of it, silent,
waiting, full.

The hand is barnboard, hay bales stacked
against the shed and the dug-out gullies and ditches,
waist-high in weeds.
The hand is shadow and light,
a delicate screen of leaf.

The hand is broken glass, hawk talon, blood,
bone and nerve. The hand is bread.

The hand is dust, is longing in the dust, is fine,
long-fingered, is heat
from the pitch of the crow's sleek back
and the howl of a coyote pack.

The hand is lust, is life.

The hand is the small brown wren picking its way
across the stones on the path.
The hand is familiar, transient, bold,
is what is left
when the heart has had its fill.

Listening to Mozetich in the Parking Lot

– after Marjan Mozetich, *Affairs of the Heart,*
Concerto for Violin and String Orchestra

Not only a grip-your-waist bass
to hold up an entire breaking sky,
but harmonies suspended
like great slow-winged birds,
slow enough to turn
your insides out,
but moving still
to somewhere
past what you can see.
If you sit here long enough,
the dark will take a turn with you,
leave you out of breath, in rags
and dumb.
Only breathe
and ask for more.
Only sing.

Muse

In that vague, refracted, double life of dream,
the baby hawk, clinging to my finger by its beak,
was you: the small, tight body,
heavier than it seemed at first
and heavier as it clung, was yours.
I swung my arm out more than once to shake you off,
more than once you held,
but when I swung out hard against the wall
and finally, I saw there was no wound,
you'd left no mark. And my hand,
dumb with beating and a cracked and sombre weight,
seemed only echo,
aftersense of hand.

That Other Beauty

When the small boy's eyes are brown and pleading,
and the enemy is standing to the side, smiling
at your voice about to falter, give way,
you ask yourself, is this the strangeness then,
that other beauty?

And packs of crows strain the air with screaming,
the road is wet with grief, but you give in, lie down lovely with it,
new light falling on your hands, your feet, the leaves too,
falling pale and perfect in a desiccated air.

That other beauty singing past the angry crowds,
the borders of your little town, amid the dust,
dirt and traffic signs—all the gestures
pointing to a mapped and censored way.
You hear so much,

and then the candles with their thin flames in the window
burning low and lower as the shadows on the wall become a wall
themselves. You know it's close.
The flame sucked in and with that blue release of wick
and heat—incandescence.
Your eyes alive with sound.

The Furnace Cleaner

He stands there, blackened, with a grateful eye.
It's late, she says, you must be tired,
but I want to tell you this:
when I called to set a time, the woman's voice,
it must have been your wife,
reminded me of winter bells,
the way the sound draws circles on your skin,
shadows over snow,
the clarity.

And he goes home to wash
the furnace soot from his spare face, long hands,
and over supper in the kitchen,
listens to a dark-haired woman,
taken in. With his finger
traces circles on her arm.
And the night air through the window,
and the maples, leafless,
shaking in a northern wind.

The Grocer's Son

The corner market opens early, the sun still low,
still orange. The flower lady sets out tulip pails,
pots of mums, begonias, asian lilies
wrapped in paper cones. Most days
she rolls the awning down for shade.
It's heavy work—the turn and clank
or when the canvas catches—
but her husband's in the back unloading vegetables,
the older son, the tall one,
manages the cash.

Someday, this will all be his.
For now he works beside a student in the afternoons,
a girl who cycles down from music class in sweats,
never wearing underwear
or so it seems,
her hair at a loss after all that wind,
knuckles chapped. Sometimes, packing bags,
her thigh will brush against his leg, her eyes
move sideways, but the grocer's son is steady,
eyes on the future like a dark horse
judging distance, pace,
remembered rise.

5 a.m.

You stand in last year's cornfield
with a suitcase in your hand.
A borrower? A lucky find?
But no, the suitcase is yours, heavy
with the old heaviness.
Still, you shake with fear—
someone will see you, think it is stolen.
In the half-light, a slowing car. You run
but the headlights catch the case, glinting.
You run faster, shift its weight to the other hand,
but the beam is unrelenting, reeling,
like the suitcase in your hand—
heart pounding, as the load
you carry, stolen or not, just shines
and shines and shines.

Early Morning

And Mahler is weeping all over the dash.
I am lost to the world. For so long it has heard nothing from me.
Oboes, horns, the sky a rack of blue and early morning traffic starting up.
And then that turn of phrase to gather the lovely pulse in its palm
and tighten: *I live alone.*
The sky opens to whiteness.

A painter at the crossing for the bus, slumped forward,
stained from his cap to his steel-toed boots,
all the weight of his long-muscled days held bare
in the circles under his eyes.
To put a hand to his jaw, just now,
to turn his face with only fingertips, to ask
if it's the being lost that counts.
We look for the empty room, the square of light on the bare wood floor,
echoes from the walls. We look for the chair by the window,
the one cup, the coat.
And then that momentary lifting into air,
the view, the weightlessness of arms conducting sound in gestures
larger than shadow or light,
when the turn of phrase is everything,
that slow spinning,
pulse to face to sky
and back again.

The Smallest Thing

It wasn't that he looked at her with warmth
or tenderness. He often looked away.
It wasn't that they read each other's minds—
there she drew a blank—
or that he needed her.

It was the unrelenting line of his jaw,
a certain stillness in his gestures,
and once, walking on the bridge,
he put his hand
flat against her back,
the lowest part,
and there were lilacs.

Dan's Market, Oldfield Road

Wanting to savour,
in the shade of the market,
the moment of warm fruit, the fact
of standing upright, my working eyes.

Look, I want to say to all the others
in amongst the crates,
this is passing, this moment
of peach and melon, radishes,
the birds in their cages wanting more;
even as we mull, the stalks of corn against the wall
are mute and browning, leaning
so the side-light catches
only now. Tiny sounds of lambs
are being lost in air.

That winter of leaving.
One day. At noon.
How the light through the vines
at the dining room window
moved across the ironing board
in patterns. How the stairs
needed washing.

Cat

It isn't mine, said the man next door,
meaning the cat lying dead on his lawn,
the flies on its open eyes, the teeth,
the ears, and then the grass
padded down as if it took awhile.

Meaning too, death is not owned.
Not the child's hand raised high in class:
I know, I know. Or the man in a crowded room
guiding a woman with his arm around her waist
stopping here and there to ask,
Have you met my wife?

Death is the hand snapped away from the stove,
the door shut tight against an icy wind,
towels rolled up against the cracks.

At a Party

She talks to me of cassava,
this woman from Nigeria. Long story,
everything a distance and her dark, shining eyes.
How the hands are used as if the pot were here in front of us,
the smell, the taste. How the fingers work, the thumbs.
In her soft words, rhythmic
with the beat of markets, music, clay:
another kind of light, another heat.
I am a stranger there.
But the woman from Nigeria knows nothing of the fields,
the small stones and orchards of my place.
She knows nothing of the willow trees,
white birch, cicadas in the leaves.
We have only this exchange
to draw each other in.
Cassava, a mango here,
here a firefly.
Almonds, cinnamon, the village dust;
then again, crickets in July,
lilacs bursting off the barn.
The rest is heart to heart,
the need for home, for place,
for what the hands are doing,
the language of the shining eyes.

Gathering

The neighbour's backyard party noise
moves in waves, sun-dappled.
Across the street the other neighbours
welcome friends: more laughter, potluck night.
Someone drops a plate. Thin screams.
A cough. Everywhere
this closing in—
a gathering of ghosts,
the curtain's folly,
voices in the walls.

Desire

You are not loved. Such clarity
of green against the sun-cut fields, such heat.
And smacking air—the bending,
crackling air is making room for something bigger,
something you've forgotten in the night.
You can't go back. This close to the long breath
is a violence. Everywhere the lion's low crouch,
the stink of mane, everywhere a locking door.
Only swallows lift off from the tinder beams.
See them rising
into fixed and sombre air.

Foresight

You will leave them knowing this: there will be winters
when the snow will turn its hands
around the darkest trees, the longest fields.
There will be crying in the woods, a sun so late,
so low, it will seem held
in the limit of its strange yellow light.
There will be absence, days of listening for a breath,
a voice come home to sing,
and nights without a single open door.
And years will pass, turn over
after you, and they will wait it out,
carry with them only small things claiming you:
a painted jar, a notebook, shell, a scarf,
and something without name: your shoulders
breaking through the edges of their sightlines,
leaning into middle distance, bare white sound,
your shoes pressing into earth, just here
and here, here,
as you walk on,
leaving them.

II

Contemplation: Three Panels

Deep snow. A listless, pale sun.
The quiet want of winter's lying in.
At McNab, the steeple clears the gully bush
and skeins of long white sky unroll as far as you can see.
Strands of poplar break the line, and oak
and elm. This is the place you come to
for the end of flat-handed light.
See the circling hawk: there is longing here,
a brush stroke in the trick of wind lifting off the drifts
and settling back. And lifting.

....

Mourn for the hollow where your boot has broken through,
the thrust and give, and nothing but whiteness on this plain.
You need the stalks of ragweed,
red-brown winter char, you need the fall-off sky.
The world narrows with your breath,
widens with the heart's long leaning into wind,
pulse of belonging and then not.
Bird tracks like remembered songs,
scattered, without end.

....

Hymn to the winter orchard's giving in.
The trail is covered over, blank space between the apples,
pears, between the sumac and the ridge of breaking plums.

Dark branches hold the sky's grey weight
and less than that: the dots of swallows homing in,
last offerings before the bank, the lake's slow claim.
The sun seems closer here and if you look out past the Welland locks,
to where the concrete buttments channel into shallow ice,
you can see the end of what this is.
The name eludes you.
And the silence—dream stripped down to its essential grain,
the eye's unbearable scan.

Other Worlds

You claim these cold, still fields
until the calls of nesting killdeer
seem, not echo, but a shadow on the snow line.
From rows of grapevines on the wires,
blackened anchor posts, you take the long-eyed distance,
walk the line between necessity
and something less defined again.

And who will guide you through the streets,
the terrible grid of mathematic fact, when the air
is thick with ash and the heat of crowds jostling for a place,
when the lanterns hanging in the trees,
as if from nothing, aren't enough,
and there is no space for you, your lion heart,
the stones still heavy in your pockets,
the measure in your mind of other worlds,
globed and without light.

Sparrows

Tuesday and the two men and a bit of bread.
The river's edge just there and sparrows coming early in the day.
One man puts his arm out and they gather, dip and poke
at the sleeve of his pale grey suit, pick crumbs
from his long open hand.
The other man looks out to the hills, still dark
across the river's edge, a sparrow sitting
in the fold of his hat.
They are old, these men. The bench is worn.
Tuesday early and they bring their bread and sparrows dance.
What is this slowness in their hands, their feet, what stillness here?
What refuge in the purple hills?
Another Tuesday then, another time, a door is opened
and they shuffle out in rags to smoke and shouts,
in dust they shuffle to a clearing, two of them,
to watch the smoke lift with their yellowed eyes,
see the heavy lifting of the day.
And a sparrow there, sitting
on a branch of the one tree left, leafless,
a single apricot hanging in the light,
blinding them with orange.

Train Station, Moscow, 1929

They tie the children to each other
by their wrists, two here, two there,
to keep them close.
And hollow faces, crowds.
On the benches sit the lesser gods
in uniform, splitting seeds
between their teeth.
Sunflower seeds. (And past the village gates in June
there were plum trees; by the river, oaks;
the churchyard blooming.)
The iron bars of sewer grates
are strewn with shells.

Leaving Zaporozhye

Old men weeping and the women carry bread
to a nickled sun. Weeds grow from their eyes, long tears.
Children singing songs of wood and ash,
mouthing every other word.

The rivers have run dry. Stones that pressed
their stories deep into the riverbed
lean hard on silence now. Moved.

And in the linings of their coats the white-haired girls
sew grey feathers, bits of polished glass,
red-breasted birds and willow canes.
Needles, thread of bone.

There is darkness in the boots that have no soles.
To walk this far on skin. On skin to wager
and on flight: the swift, black exodus of crows.

Confession

I want, in this shaking wind, to move,
be moved. I want a shaking heart.

And wild horses heading toward the light,
and magpies wheeling in the trees.

Electric air: catch and singe my throat.
My ears are filled with open-flowered song.

I've come this far on limbs of birch and pear,
the psalms of trilliums, wood-lit,

on the blossomed bones of words. In my hands
the empty bowl of luck is glazed with ash.

I've heard the weeping in the streets. I've seen the martyrs,
marble-eyed, watching from their shallow forest graves.

And when the rooms were bare and windowless,
and the winds came with their black rain and the darkness

and the coats on nails like frameless men,
the pockets hollow-mouthed, I wanted this:

to see the shape of things completely,
every darkness, every rise and fall, small breath.

I've looked to the hills a hundred times
and a hundred more and watched the strands of gulls,

reeling, belly-white, delivered.
The sun has forced its course on me,

the long-patterned trees, the shadow-vines.
And in my mind's eye too, a dipping and a turning:

an irised ring, open to the elements
and light.

Port Elgin

I remember us standing by the lake,
the fuchsia bathing suit, a chill to bring September on,
low clouds, but the three of you went in,
and afterwards the cottage warm,
listening to Brahms or was it Schubert?
I've forgotten now.
We were all transfixed by music then,
so many four-hand gatherings, such talk
of phrasing and voice, the intricate articulations
of a language given over, hook and line,
to wordlessness, gestures in the air.
But the sun set over the lake, I do remember that—
how the sky had changed somehow
through dinner, how the sun came out and finally,
a brilliant orange that settled it, and pinks and yellows
banked across the view beyond our chairs.
We didn't know that time would move much faster
after that. We didn't see it coming, somehow,
caught there as we were, symphonically,
one blazing hour of our lives,
the sun dropping down into the lake in front of us,
not a word said
and our heads moving slightly
with the rise and fall of violins.

Varieties of Light

If you could be everywhere.
If you could lie down over the world
and cover its dark, lonely living with your own dark heart.
If the people on the street, the children skipping,
old men and their walking sticks,
could breathe in one breath, deeply,
and the faces of strangers, lovers, friends,
could be one face, cut fine
against a close, clear sky,
you would know the bones behind the eye,
the pupil's deep flint.
But what you know is like the pulsing leaf-light
from the window of the bus, patterns
slashed across your eyelids, loss you're blinded by,
then not, and changing every quarter-blink.
What you know are only fragments of a glare,
varieties of light, thin dreams
that catch the blade of splendour.

Innocence

Stopped at the light and a young man
sitting on the sidewalk with a jar for coins
and his sign propped up. *Lonely. Out of work.*
What's to stop me putting out a hand
and reaching for his sleeve, his face?
I can almost hear him breathe, he's close enough.
Through the window, rolled down,
he can hear my radio,
and if I looked to the left, I'd see his eyes,
full-on, wondering at my ability
or inability to cross the desert line, the no man's land,
to some remembrance of a starting point,
the tiny foot in air, the bawling need.
And so I wait here for the light to change,
the greenest heart between us beating
through the metal door, the pull of it,
the leaves, the light, my knee against the door, the rush,
the question of my knowing this,
the question of his.

Shadows on the Roof

Slow rain again and softly,
softly knocking on the door.
The gulls are sullen with the sound, a sinking
long in darkness, open-mouthed, and moss
accepting weight without its grain. We know
no better here. No more or less.
A movement in the firs like breathing
and the first stunned limb of night
breaks through the crest, the first call
from the bones of trees becomes a hollow stone,
the shell of light, a moon.
To wait for something closer now,
something drawing in: a raven
gives itself to the clear, bright density of rain,
to the sound of our hands
beating back the wash
as the trees lean into nothingness,
their branches bleeding light.

Sunflowers

Deluge of bird calls, squirrel chat.

Sound of water moving through the culverts
in the clutch and dodge of earth.

They're taking down the trees just past the ridge,
shattering this afterglaze of light,
the steady insect drone.

You reel it in.

If you could hear a single intonation without waver,
pause for breath, if you could hear one treble line,
thought accurately poised—

but you are tired now,
your voice moving into shallow sand.

                    Sunflowers—
growing up the side of the barn so bright
you shield your eyes and still,
through your thin-skinned hands,
you see the blaze.

Church Job: Day One

Just fifteen.
You've pulled out all the stops:
diapason, dulcet, vox,
geigen, flauto, hautboy, horn.
Fingers splay the manuals,
legs the easy octave,
couplers on. One chord
to set the pitch, you're onto it.
Nothing missing but the signal from above.
He's up there now: a modern Moses at the pulpit,
white-haired, arms stretched high, palms out,
more divine aim than a forked willow branch
and the flock of four hundred
rising to their feet.
Momentarily the signal blurs, fogs up.
Palms out or down?
Must be out. You let her rip.
All the rage of wood and steel in thirty-two foot pipes,
a rush of air to bring down Sinai stone
and you're surging into absolute vibrato,
bells and sound of cello, trumpet, bass,
a chord to counter hell.
Then that sweep of elbow,
wrist, the final flourish
off the cuff.
Magnificent.
Pure swell.
But no one has their hymnals out
and Moses looks down
resolute, says softly,
Let us pray.

Pruning the Apple Tree

My brother in his coveralls,
pruning shears in hand, says, Think of this as art.
He starts removing all the winter kill,
the new green suckers shooting up the trunk,
and with his wide hands on the branches
says, Now feel the shape. Imagine it.
He fingers the end buds.
Here's the place, and here,
and while I watch him it makes sense—
how he leaves the biased cuts
like tiny points of orphaned light,
white words, facing out.

Unaccompanied Bach

The mind's wilderness.
Enormous silence smashed against collage.
Not one word.
And the need for something resolute,
a single melody to bear the weight,
a dark, liquid spin.

Poverty

Cello of interrupted light, low ravishment,
leaves a play of shadow-palms, a sifting
close and thin. How to trust the separations
after this beguiling: resonance of resonance,
the dark heart's perfect pitch, dark
within the dark. How to trust the endless layers
of resist and shift, the crossroad heave. At every turn
the overhang of your attention gives you one more chance
to get it right, take in something given.
Eye to the hummingbird's glittering eye,
hand to the lion's mouth,
the desert voice, the a cappella riff.

III

Before

It was a time of watching from the window,
the poplars never still, the fence going on.
A time of quiet offerings: the oriole nest
suspended in the dying elm, the shed,
and fields of goldenrod and cabbages
burning in the sun. We trusted then
that the dog would dodge the wheel,
that the tractor coming to the end of the row
would make a perfect arc and miss the first tree of the next,
that ploughed-up soil would be dark in spring, the wells too,
dark and full. We moved our hands
around the long-smoothed handles of hoes,
the wood of baskets, ladders, crates,
and that other older wood: the broad, black limbs
of cherry and pear, unyielding as rock
or stone or God and there was order then.
A solemn turning over of what must, what
should, what would be done.
Eyes on the line of trees meeting sky.
Humming, sometimes silence.
And the tar would bubble up with heat
on the lake road going out, and you and I would walk
until our shoes were black with it
and sticking, the distant line
still distant.

Hoeing Strawberries

Turning up the earth with smooth, deft strokes,
or in dry heat and weeks
of promised rain, the grate of a metal blade
against the crust. And I remember
long, low fields of strawberries in bloom,
the three of us, bare-legged, kerchiefed, shirts
tied tight around our waists, the click of hoes
hooking if we got too close, laughter,
and the day and distance measured by the sycamores,
the drainage ditch, how close the water can and lunch.
Time stretched only as far as the end of the row.
Past the rise, the lake:
just out of reach and cool.

Notes on the Angel's Descent

Listening for a friction of the thinnest kind,
you put your ear to the world.
Blue dragonflies and hummingbirds explode.
Herons lift from bottomless ponds.

What is the most you can ask of air?
Distance, the impartiality of water
emptied of its darker, reedy drift,
the clarity of music without sound.

In the bright grip of leaves, you're tempted
by the hand that takes you back to streamlined silence,
ash, the months of night,
cinder of your self.

You wait for the moon's pale given,
a whitening of birch, sudden breath.
The space between intention and its gesture
narrows into one pure beam.

Three Poems to Denman Island

Early

Your shadow is so thin.
You move among the rock and fern,
a single reed. A note.
Intonation of the self.

On the Third Day

Ritual: the well-swept floor,
the teacup in your hand
and rain, rain.

Cottage

Potted geraniums
line the deck
and mister frog
plays the double bass,
his stone bow
unmoved.
And shifting firs and dark,
unfathomable greens.

Tuning

Under a raked sky
the trees are bare,
the fields a long-shaped grey.
Afterlight: a bell of cold to catch the flicker's
bright back, the flint of hawk.
The mind takes it in like a compound eye,
seeing, turning, seeing,
listening for the central pitch.
And resonance.
And form.
And unblinking thought.

Entering

In half-light now, a thickening—
                    grey boarded barn
and swallows arcing dust and echo up above the pulleys,
windlessness, old wood,
a possibility of weight, the air tan-smoked;
                    so too, the voices,
layers of them coming from the slats.
And in the one high window, cracked,
the ladder leading to it halfway up the wall,
a shaft of noon—
                    behind you,
grass to the stoop thigh-high
and sudden drench of willow.

Everything Spoken For

Even the green heat
and the last legs of the grasses,
all the gnarled sweetness in the pears.
September's full-day weight
has pulled you through the length,
the breadth of light and left you squandered
on the other side.
Grains of remembering split your ear.
From the far fields, a sediment
of ripening: must of haying, dry mud flats,
the last of the currants left to winter and drip.
And bands of sheep, so small
and thoughtful, grey,
keepers of a radiant dawn.
Sleepless now,
you hang your heart
where it belongs.

Retreat

And morning.
Gravel tamps beneath your feet,
lungs regain their shape.
Breathe deeply. And again.
Take in the damp, the wood-smelling vines,
take in the green of cedars breathing.
This place is large enough.
Sway, white birch—
the wheeze, the sigh,
and then wisteria,
the world.

Highway Turn

The heat of the day is on you now,
a slow noon singeing in the glare, flat gold
of ragweed, thistle, wind as dry as whistling grass
and then cicadas, blasting through the orchard pears.
Everywhere the pulse of what you know
and what you don't: a rising shimmer coming off the road
as you head for the highway turn.

No rain in weeks and all you need is one voice
naming you, taking the stain on your hands,
your feet hard with dirt, one voice
turning the beat in your ears to something held
quiet, cool, offered in shade
to the wide open mouth of your heart,
and you will stay.
You will stay.

Magnetic Field

To find the magnet's lone north end.
To split and resplit infinitely
in search of pure beginning's
pure beginning.

And loss. With every definition
we lose a kind of faith in the underlife,
the something not known but believed,
barely felt, but felt,
barely heard, but heard,
the invisible weight in the palm of the hand
that sings its own lilting song.

Physics

Gravity is relative, he says,
as a fixed idea, doesn't exist.
He says there's actually a dip in space,
pulling everything in.
Apparent force, he says.
So the apple's fall is not a fall
but something more like wish—
our feet, when walking, meet the earth by chance,
the spine a wicker weight
against the lure.
It explains this constant leaning into nothingness,
our attachment to stars,
the one shameless moon.

Pausing on the Icy Step in November

You have no language for this cold,
the insidious hands that press the clear ice plate
across your face.

Brown leaf: I have no language
for this seeing—you, still-framed—
against the knowing, days ago,
of wind, the sky-long skeins,
your whistling spirit life.

Old Man

He walks the same streets every day.
His shopping cart is piled high with plastic bags
filled with other plastic bags and in them,
others still. He ties the ends with string.
Some days I see him waiting for the bus
and wonder how that works: the cart,
the bags, his filthy beard.
Every day a gathering, the journey
heavy with his load.
Every day a life.

Gordon Point

And then the full moon split the strait.
I stood there looking past the firs, arbutus—
black against that shine—and faced its open mouth.
Hours of that night.
And houses of the city at my back, street lights
up the hill, insect beds electric in the weeds.
I could have put my hand out for the current there.
And no one came. No one
saw me standing at the brink,
about to trade one orbit for another.

The Last Passage

You find it under the shelf of earth where the give
gives way to something hard and known,
unconquerable. Dream's bright axis
in the dark, discovered whole and fugitive.
Trees hang over you like death,
and fear comes lean and quick from a brittle north.
To push through roots as old as myth
and precious stone, grammar by grammar,
plane by plane, to an undiluted core
is the final rite, and more than what's been offered
in the other world, now adrift, where geese
are leaving light behind them in great bands
and starlings, stung
with a force of wind
years in the making,
ravel and dive.

Wisdom

It is in the persistent unfolding,
what we barely believe,
in half-life: part shadow, the opening phrase
of the *lied* and only that,
delicate movements of wrens
just seen
in the lower leaves.
This is the edge, papery thin
and it's all we have.
But you already know this, you
who walk softly under the pink, blossoming trees.

Bearers of Wisdom

We come with nothing but the old words
carried in our smooth, white arms.
Stars flower in our mouths.
And the man walking through the empty streets
asking questions of us all,
what gift for him?
One word—grace, or beauty,
love—one word
and he will weep, this man
who wanders loose-kneed, open-palmed,
among the ruins.

Solitude

Everything you can and cannot have is here.
You see it spread in front of you, flat and sensible
and huge, and watch the light divide things
carefully: the distant from the near, the vibrant
from the pale, smooth from frayed,
the wind-blown from the still.
It's the best you can do, this watching,
and putting your hands out now and then
through charged blue air as if your fingers,
to remember what's been claimed, what not,
need only graze the edge.

Acknowledgments

I am deeply grateful to Jan Zwicky for her editing and encouragement, and to Patrick Lane for his support. A special thanks, too, to Amalie Enns, Diane Enns and Dexine Wallbank for conversation and comment.

To the editors of *The Fiddlehead, The Antigonish Review, PRISM international, Grain Magazine* and *The Malahat Review*, who first published versions of several of these poems, my sincere appreciation.

Karen Enns is from southern Ontario, where she was born and raised in a Mennonite farm community. Her poetry has appeared in *The Fiddlehead*, *The Antigonish Review*, *Grain Magazine*, *PRISM international* and *The Malahat Review*. She lives in Victoria, B.C.